Lake Placid circa 1928

On the forested edge of Lake Placid, in the shadow of Whiteface Mountain,

a small hotel looks out over the water. An old Adirondack lodge of arching cedar branches,

smooth painted pine, and diamond-paned windows. A traditional, personal hotel,

gracious and firelit, with views to take your breath away.

This is Lake Placid Lodge.

L A K E   P L A C I D   L O D G E

The dusky forests of the great Adirondacks spread over New York state like a cape. It is an ancient wild place, six million acres of wilderness, bigger than Yellowstone, Grand Canyon and Yosemite combined. The round shining lakes still hidden like coins high up in the mountains were left behind by four separate ice ages, the scattered change of glaciers. The first to inhabit this wooded eden were animals in abundance: wolves and bears, mountain lions and moose. They ruled the forest for millennia and dipped their heads to the tumbling snowmelt rivers. After them came Algonquin and then Iroquois, and by the 18th century, European trappers had discovered the beavers and mink of the North Woods.

Lakefront cabins

THE ADIRONDACK STATE PARK IS COMPRISED OF 6 MILLION ACRES OF WILDERNESS, 46 MOUNTAINS OVER 4000 FEET, 31,500 MILES OF RIVERS AND 2300 LAKES AND PONDS, THAT MUST REMAIN "FOREVER WILD."

"The kind of dreamy place where a rowboat signifies adventure and the cry of loons provides a little night music."

Diversion Magazine

*Whiteface Mountain
and Lake Placid*

AUTUMN IN THE ADIRONDACKS IS THE TIME
WHEN THE SALMON RUN, AND THE BIRD AND
BIG GAME SEASONS BEGIN. THE ADIRONDACK
PARK HAS 50 SPECIES OF MAMMALS,
220 SPECIES OF BIRDS, 66 SPECIES OF FISH,
AND 2500 MILES OF FOOT TRAILS
ON WHICH TO FIND THEM.

The settlers who came to these rugged mountains after the American Revolution were Vermonters pushing westward to what was then the wild frontier. Using only what they found in the woods – tree trunks and birch bark, branches and stones – they built small cabins and filled them with furniture they made with an ax and their own tough hands. The first camps were crude, but as they evolved, enormous stone fireplaces were built for heat and porches laid out for fine weather. The new craft and architecture of the woods was so striking, so unique, that it became known as "the Adirondack style."

Attracted by the handsome, rustic cabins and the endless forests at a time when wilderness was fast disappearing, the millionaires of the Industrial Age descended upon the Adirondacks to build their summer retreats. Mansions of log and stone sprang up on the edges of the high clear northern lakes, and trainloads of wealthy visitors – nannies, footmen, champagne and silver in tow – came north to "rough it" every August. The era of the Great Camps had begun.

Near the heart and center of these wide woods is Lake Placid. It is an old lake, deep and pure, five miles from end to end and strewn with leafy islands. The surface is sometimes so still and shining it could be taken for polished stone. Whiteface Mountain towers above, nearly a mile high.

"Here the notion of escape endures. It's defined by cool morning air, deep vistas, and silence broken only by the trickle of an oar cutting through a mirror lake, the snap of a twig, the hoot of an owl."

Travel & Leisure

THE JACK RABBIT TRAIL IS A 25-MILE CROSS-COUNTRY SKI TRAIL NAMED FOR "JACK RABBIT" JOHANNSEN, A SKIING PIONEER WHO LIVED TO AGE 111. THE TRAIL LINKS KEENE, LAKE PLACID AND SARANAC LAKE, PASSING BY THE LODGE'S FRONT DOOR, AND WILL EVENTUALLY EXTEND TO TUPPER LAKE, WITH OVER 60 MILES OF UNBROKEN SKIING.

In 1882, a German family built a camp at the edge of the lake – a perfect spot, they thought – for on the high bank, in the sweet piney air, you could sit all day and watch Whiteface admire its own mighty reflection in the water. They gave their camp grand proportions: tall stone fireplaces, diamond-paned windows, long twig-framed porches that faced the glorious view.

Here friends and family would come to stay for a month or a season, and the days were filled with shouting fun and long tramps through the fragrant woods, and the nights with firelit stories and wool blankets tucked over knees. It was a life both rustic and splendid. Today the old camp is an inn, a traditional, personal hotel of arching cedar branches and smooth painted pine, with seventeen rooms and suites and seventeen snug cabins at the water's edge. A hotel in the spirit of the Great Camps, of luxury and celebration hidden away in the quiet woods.

"I understand why these mountains are forever wild. The law has something to do with it. So do the people. But it's winter that keeps it honest."

Travel Holiday

LAKE PLACID WAS THE SITE OF THE 1932 AND
1980 WINTER OLYMPICS; AND IN FACT
INTRODUCED WINTER SPORTS TO AMERICA IN
1904, WITH SKIING AND ICE-SKATING AT THE
LAKE PLACID CLUB.

Stairway to the Moose Sitting Room

Lake Placid Lodge still feels like a private camp, its rooms filled with art, antiques and Oriental rugs. The chairs and desks and tables, the paintings on the walls, have all been handmade by local artisans. As if a path into some secret forest, a grand, tree-lined stairway leads down to the Moose Sitting Room, where the fireplace is always blazing and the windows frame the glittering lake. Just beyond is the pub, a place to sit and have a pint of stout or a whiskey, study

"…Lake Placid Lodge…a balance between comfortable rusticity and first-rate amenities

all in an Arcadian lakefront setting…"

Departures Magazine

IN 1985, A TROUT WEIGHING IN AT 32 POUNDS WAS CAUGHT IN LAKE PLACID. IT WAS THE LARGEST LAKE TROUT TAKEN IN THE CONTINENTAL U.S. SINCE 1919.

the old photographs on the walls and have the barkeep recount a story or two. In the game room upstairs you'll find a billiards table, board games, perhaps a puzzle, half-solved, spread out across a table. Sit in a wicker armchair out on the wide porch to watch the sun rise, cruise the lake in a classic antique boat or glide a canoe out into the lavender half-light of evening.

"Lake Placid Lodge...built on a hillside overlooking one of the most serene lake and mountain views in North America..."

New York Magazine

The Lodge has a dining room that features new American cuisine with distinct Adirondack flavors – local vegetables and wild mushrooms, game and fowl, whatever is best and freshest that day. The menu changes with the seasons, and is complemented by a list of award-winning wines ranging from the modest to the illustrious. Food is a focal point at the Lodge, and many people plan their stay around the dining room. But the staff can also pack you a gourmet lunch if you'd rather take to the trails or even dine in a canoe in the middle of the lake.

OCCASIONALLY, ONE CAN SEE STRANGE PROTUBERANCES ON VERY OLD TREES. WHEN THESE HUGE OLD PINES WERE SAPLINGS, IROQUOIS YOUTHS WOULD PROVE THEIR STRENGTH BY TWISTING AND TYING THEM INTO KNOTS.

"We had the rare, pleasant, died-and-went-to-heaven feeling that only comes when every aspect of a meal is perfectly on target."

Metroland

From your table, branches on the ceiling seem to frame a dark and starry sky, as if you were seated on the forest floor. The walls in the dining room are carved with woodland scenes, and the very chair you sit in was created, traditionally, out of materials found in the woods. On summer evenings, tables ablaze with candlelight and crystal are set out on the porch, where the music is the singing of the crickets and the frogs.

Herb Crusted Rack of Lamb

PAUL SMITH, A FAMOUS ADIRONDACK HOTELIER IN THE 1900S, WAS SO RENOWNED FOR HIS WRY HUMOR THAT A MAN COULD EARN A DRINK BY RECOUNTING SMITH'S LATEST JOKE.

"The dining room is intimate and woodsy, and the menu — exemplary American cuisine featuring fresh local delicacies — is up to the level of a Manhattan five-star restaurant."

New York Magazine

WHITEFACE MOUNTAIN, THE SITE OF THE
1932 & 1980 WINTER OLYMPICS, HAS THE
GREATEST VERTICAL DROP EAST OF THE
MISSISSIPPI (3,216 FT.)

*Our famous raconteur, former bobsled champion and
U.S. Olympic team manager, "Dew Drop" Morgan*

In the wine cellar, marvelous private dinners are served. You may choose your vintages right from the shelves, and toast the day's adventures. A meal served in the wine cellar is always a celebration, be it a birthday, a mountain scaled, or just the good fortune of being there together. You might plan a menu with the chef to touch upon favorite flavors, or order a tasting menu and see what imaginative dishes arrive at the table.

*"Lake Placid Lodge – a century-old camp restored to the splendor of
the Great Camp tradition."*

Adirondac

"Award of Excellence"
Wine Spectator

IN THE 1880S, P.T. BARNUM WAS IMPRESSED BY A TRIO OF LARGE, VERY TALL BROTHERS, ALL GUIDES IN THE LAKE PLACID AREA, AND OFFERED THEM PAID POSITIONS AT HIS CIRCUS AS THE "ADIRONDACK GIANTS." THE OFFER WAS INDIGNANTLY REFUSED.

The Den

Downstairs, next to the wine cellar, there are spacious, airy meeting rooms, wide-open porches, and another sitting area – a cozy, firelit place where you can pull a book from the shelves and take your time about the afternoon. Outside on the upper porch, stout wicker armchairs might soon become a habit, with the outdoor hearth ablaze and the lake lit up like fire.

"While many alpine retreats offer charming fireside settings, only a few offer true warmth. Travelers find more than just a roaring fire at the Lake Placid Lodge – gracious hospitality, distinctive amenities and unforgettable dining."

Northeast Physician

The guests' accommodations are the heart of Lake Placid Lodge. The feeling of the rooms, suites and cabins is of a private place, a camp of one's own, warm and comfortable, tucked beneath the high swaying trees, safe from wind and weather. Each and every one is spacious, luxurious, imaginative; rich with soft fabrics, polished wood, tall stone fireplaces, views of silver lake or shadowy firs. Each is supremely comfortable, and entirely individual. No two are the same.

NEARBY FOLLENSBY POND WAS NAMED AFTER A STRANGE BRITISH HERMIT WHO LIVED ALONE ON THE EDGE OF THE POND. AFTER HIS DEATH A CENTURY AGO, PAPERS WERE FOUND IN HIS LITTLE CABIN THAT SUGGESTED ROYAL BIRTH AND A UNKNOWN CRIME COMMITTED AGAINST HIM. BUT HIS REAL NAME, HIS PAPERS, AND EVEN THE SITE OF HIS GRAVE HAVE SINCE BEEN LOST.

"Lake Placid Lodge is loaded with comfortably deep tubs, dreamy beds, cedar closets."

Travel & Leisure

Hearthside Guest Room

"THE HABIT OF CALLING VILLAGES (AFTER) LAKES, WHEN THEY ARE OFTEN NOT EVEN ON THE WATERS WHOSE NAME THEY SHARE, IS A MARKED PECULIARITY OF ADIRONDACK NOMENCLATURE."

ALFRED L. DONALDSON

Whiteface Suite deck

The thirty-four guest rooms and cabins, named for the region's high peaks and lakes, are filled with rustic twig and birch bark furniture, Adirondack antiques, Oriental carpets, featherbeds, and artwork created by local artisans. A room might have a huge fireplace in a stone alcove filling an entire wall. An archway made of branches leading to a quiet sunlit sitting room. A big red armchair with a tapestried ottoman. Most rooms and cabins have porches or stone-floored patios, and Adirondack chairs for reading in, with a minute stolen every so often to look up at the view.

"As romantic as sleeping beneath the stars."

Diversion Magazine

Pinnacle Guest Room

The seventeen cabins are a world unto themselves. They are a short walk under a covered walkway from the lodge – the farthest being about 350 yards – and are grouped along the edge of the clear, pebble-bottomed lake. Set beside the Whiteface Club, they are as large and luxurious as the Lodge suites, and uncommonly comfortable, with beamed ceilings, stone fireplaces, walk-in closets, big sturdy beds piled with down pillows. Each cabin feels like a home in the woods, thick-walled and firelit, with picture windows that gaze out over the lake to the mountains.

Whiteface Mountain

WHITEFACE MOUNTAIN REMINDED THE VANDERBILT FAMILY SO MUCH OF MOUNT FUJI, AND ADIRONDACK LAKES LOOKED TO THEM SO VERY JAPANESE, THAT THEY HIRED JAPANESE WORKMEN TO "JAPANIZE" THEIR CAMP ON UPPER ST. REGIS LAKE. THEY EVEN HAD THEIR MAIDS DRESS IN KIMONOS.

"Rather than being precious, the whole place leans toward unpretentious comfort."

Fortune

AUTHOR WILLIAM MURRAY TELLS OF A NEW YORKER WHO WENT TO A SARANAC LAKE HOTEL IN THE 1890'S THAT WAS SO CROWDED, EVEN THE BARN WAS OCCUPIED. THE ONLY PLACE LEFT TO SLEEP WAS ON THE POOL TABLE. IN THE MORNING, THE MAN WAS PRESENTED WITH A BILL – A DOLLAR PER HOUR HE'D SLEPT THERE – THE RATE FOR PLAYING BILLIARDS.

Lookout Cabin

Morning begins slowly, with a fold of sunlight beneath the drapes, a sigh of wind ruffling the birch trees. Make your way to the dining room, where you'll find baskets of bread baked just minutes before, jars of jam, a multitude of breakfast choices. From there, the day is yours: shape it how you wish. Take to the woods and the mountains, paddle out into the lake, lunch and white wine in a knapsack. Climb to the top of Whiteface Mountain, or wander the shops of Lake Placid, just minutes away. Sit and read in front of a softly burning fire.

"Lake Placid Lodge…Pure Adirondacks. Pure bliss."

Fortune

Whitney Cabin

Every cabin and most guest rooms have a fabulous bathroom – and sometimes two – with a tub deep enough to soak up to the neck in steaming, clear Adirondack water that was snow not long before. Most bathrooms have beadboard walls, double sinks, and glassed-in double showers. Throw open the paned windows to let in the scent of the balsam woods, or pull the drapes for privacy. Piles of thick towels and terrycloth robes are provided for your comfort.

Whiteface Suite bath

IROQUOIS INDIANS SCORNFULLY CALLED THEIR ALGONQUIN NEIGHBORS "HA-DE-RON-DAH," MEANING "TREE-EATERS." THIS UNFORTUNATE NAME WAS BASED IN TRUTH – DURING LONG, HARD WINTERS, THE ALGONQUIN WOULD EAT BARK AND TREE BUDS TO SURVIVE. THEIR ANCESTRAL LAND WAS ALSO NAMED FOR THEM: ADIRONDACK.

"Wander through tamed woods at Lake Placid Lodge – where docks are welcome mats – and launch pads – of the Adirondacks."

McKenzie Cabin

Travel & Leisure

THE WHITEFACE CLUB'S 6500-YARD GOLF
COURSE NEXT TO LAKE PLACID LODGE IS ONE
OF THE OLDEST IN THE U.S. IT WAS BUILT
IN 1896, AND THEN REDESIGNED IN 1930 BY
JOHN VANKLEEK TO HAVE GREENS AND TRAPS
IN THE SHAPE OF CLOVER LEAVES.

Biking on the Jack Rabbit Trail

There are endless things to do in and around the Lodge, though it's perfectly all right to do nothing at all. Both a historic eighteen hole golf course and four tennis courts are just steps away. There are canoes and mountain bikes available; and guides for hire can lead you up into the mountains, to find the high streams where trout gather, or the alpine meadows most favored by deer. On fine evenings, our barge sets sail around Lake Placid for a sunset cruise, and you may also rent an electric boat to explore on your own. Later, down by the edge of the lake, a bonfire is lit and s'mores and brandies are passed around, while sparks fly up into the dark sky.

"Oooh, that smell. That sweet, intoxicating fragrance of cedar and balsam pine. It's the first thing that hits you when you arrive at Lake Placid Lodge."

Bride's Magazine

Lake Placid Lodge is just on the edge of town, though the property feels secluded. Only a few minutes away lies the village of Lake Placid (which is actually on the shore of Mirror Lake). Main Street is lined with boutiques, galleries, restaurants, antique shops, and is perfectly delightful for strolling. There are museums and symphonies and exhibitions to explore. There are horse shows and trail rides, theatrical productions, and seasonal festivals. The little mountain town is bustling all year round, but in winter it really comes alive.

Home to the Winter Olympic Games in 1932 and 1980, Lake Placid continues to host world-class athletes for various competitions and events – skating, ski jumping, bobsledding, ice hockey, skiing, even dog sledding.

The Jackrabbit Trail curves right around the Lodge before it heads off into the woods again, and cross-country skiers can trace its route in winter and spring, and hikers and mountain bikers find their way when the ground is clear of snow.

"IT MAKES A MAN FEEL WHAT IT IS TO HAVE ALL CREATION UNDER HIS FEET"
– LEGENDARY GUIDE JOHN CHENEY,
AFTER THE FIRST RECORDED ASCENT
OF MT. MARCY.

"A beloved 19th-century Adirondack camp transformed…"

Diversion

ON SEPTEMBER 14, 1901, THEODORE
ROOSEVELT, VACATIONING ON MT. MARCY,
HEARD THAT PRESIDENT MCKINLEY WAS DYING
OF A GUNSHOT WOUND. ROOSEVELT RUSHED TO
MEET A TRAIN THAT WOULD TAKE HIM BACK TO
WASHINGTON, BUT UPON ARRIVING AT NORTH
CREEK STATION, HE WAS INFORMED THAT
MCKINLEY WAS DEAD, AND THAT HE,
ROOSEVELT, WAS THE NEW PRESIDENT OF
THE UNITED STATES.

Lake Placid Lodge is a hotel in the
tradition of the Adirondack Great Camps,
where the rustic, hewn-wood exteriors
contrast with the luxury and comfort within,
where the roaring fireplace and blaze of
gaiety around the table belie the hush of
falling snow; where the remote austerity of
the northern forests contrasts with the
cuisine and wines of world class dining. It's
a wonderful combination. And we would
love to have you join us.

"Live like a robber baron on retreat at Lake Placid Lodge."
Travel & Leisure, "The World's Best Awards"

Birch Lodge

DINING

The restaurant at Lake Placid Lodge, with its sweeping views of the lake and Whiteface Mountain, serves innovative cuisine with a distinct Adirondack flair, in a rustic, elegant dining room. Breakfast, lunch and dinner are served daily. Gourmet box lunches are available for trips. As the restaurant is open to the public, we strongly encourage you to make dinner reservations at the time you book your accommodations. There is no smoking in the dining room, and attire is dictated by your good taste, but we do encourage a sport coat or sweater in the evenings; and proper dress at all times in the restaurant.

Children under the age of twelve are not permitted in the dining room, due to both the tranquil, romantic atmosphere, and the sophisticated menus.

Cloudspin Conference Room

For large groups and small celebrations, the Lodge's talented staff and skilled chefs can assist you in planning an event to meet your style and budget – anything from a North Woods wedding to the ultimate dinner party can be celebrated in our private Wine Cellar or comfortable Den.

ACTIVITIES

In summer and fall, Lake Placid Lodge has a clear, sandy swimming area, and a large deck and lawn for sunbathing and relaxing. The lake itself is very clean and pure, a delight for both boaters and swimmers. Our barge departs daily from the Lodge dock for a sightseeing cruise. Nearly silent, electric Elco boats are available for rent and can carry up to four people. Old Town canoes and Cannondale mountain bikes are available at no charge. Hiking trails abound, and the High Peaks offer challenging hiking and rock climbing. Guides can be arranged for special fishing and hunting excursions. The nearby Whiteface Club has tennis courts and a championship golf course.

Come winter, excellent nordic terrain awaits on the twenty-five mile Jack Rabbit Trail, accessed from the Lodge's front door. Whiteface Mountain offers exhilarating downhill skiing. Both indoor and outdoor ice skating arenas – the largest ice complex in the world – are available for skaters of all ages in the village of Lake Placid. The Winter Olympic training sites host ski jumping competitions (winter and summer), and bobsled, luge and gondola rides are possible for anyone with the pluck to try them. For the rest of us, the Olympic Museum now offers virtual reality experiences of various Olympic events. Please ask us for a calendar of area events.

WHITEFACE CLUB RECREATION

18-hole Championship Golf: This scenic, challenging course, ringed with mountains, has wonderful views of Lake Placid and the surrounding forest. The original nine holes were built in 1898, with the second nine holes added in the 1930's by architect John VanKleek, with Walter Hagen – winner of two US Opens, four British Opens and six PGA Championships – acting as course consultant. Lessons, clinics and a half-day golf school are offered by J. Peter Martin, PGA professional.

Tennis: The Whiteface Club's eight clay tennis courts are available for guest rental. Private lessons and equipment rental can be arranged through the tennis pro.

CORPORATE RETREATS

Lake Placid Lodge has lovely conference facilities and the wooded serenity of our setting makes the Lodge the ideal place for anything from a small boardroom gathering to a week-long strategy session. The private and casual Den with a broad stone fireplace is steps away for coffee breaks, and French doors extend the meeting space outdoors to the wide stone-floored patio, where the silvery lake and Whiteface Mountain serve as backdrop.

RESERVATION INFORMATION

Please call **518-523-2700** between the hours of 9:00 a.m. and 9:00 p.m. to make a reservation. Nightly room rates are for single or double occupancy, except for our three two-bedroom lakefront cabins, which will accommodate up to four guests.

Additional guests are $100 per person, per night in rooms with pull-out sofa beds. At departure, a service charge, a New York State sales tax and an Essex County room occupancy tax will be added to your bill. The service charge allows you and your guest to enjoy a hearty Adirondack breakfast, afternoon tea service, nightly turndown service and a variety of on-site activities for each day of your stay, and include all gratuities with the exception of food and beverage services.

There is a minimum stay of two nights on weekends; while a stay of three nights is required on holidays.

Lake Placid Lodge does not own or operate the Whiteface Club.

CHILDREN

As a gentle reminder, the Lake Placid Lodge is an adult property and children above the age of twelve are most welcome. The Lodge is intended to be a quiet, romantic retreat for couples, and the menu in the dining room is geared toward adult palates. Exceptions are made when one group books the entire facility for a private party.

CHECK-IN PROCEDURES AND DEPOSITS

A one-night deposit is required for one-night stays. For two or more nights, a 50% deposit is required. Holidays require a 100% deposit. After your deposit has been received, you will be sent a letter of confirmation.

Check-in time is 4:00 p.m. Check-out is 11:30 a.m.

In keeping with our tranquil setting, there are no televisions in Lodge guest rooms. All guest rooms and our dining room are nonsmoking. Pets are welcome only in our lakefront cabins at the rate of $50 per pet, per night. There is also a $200 security deposit required for pets upon arrival, fully

Village of Lake Placid

refundable if no noise or damage issues have occurred during your stay. Pets must be on a leash at all times. Should guests leave their pet in a guest room unattended, the pet must be secured in a proper portable kennel. Guest services will not be provided in rooms where pets are unsecured.

CANCELLATIONS

Due to our intimate size, any cancellation affects us significantly. Consequently, we

adhere to the following cancellation policy:

If a cancellation is made 30 days or more prior to your arrival date, you may elect to either receive a refund of your deposit less a 10% handling fee, or apply the entire amount of your deposit toward a future stay within the next year. If your cancellation is made less than 30 days prior to your arrival date, the deposit will be forfeited.

For reservations made over holiday weekends – Martin Luther King, President's Day, Memorial Day, July 4th, Labor Day, Columbus Day, Thanksgiving, Christmas and New Year's Day – cancellations must be received at least 60 days prior to your scheduled arrival date in order to receive a refund less the 10% handling fee. If your cancellation is made less than 60 days prior to your arrival date, the deposit will be forfeited.

Should it be necessary for you to depart earlier than your confirmed dates, you will be responsible for all of the original room nights booked from your intended stay.

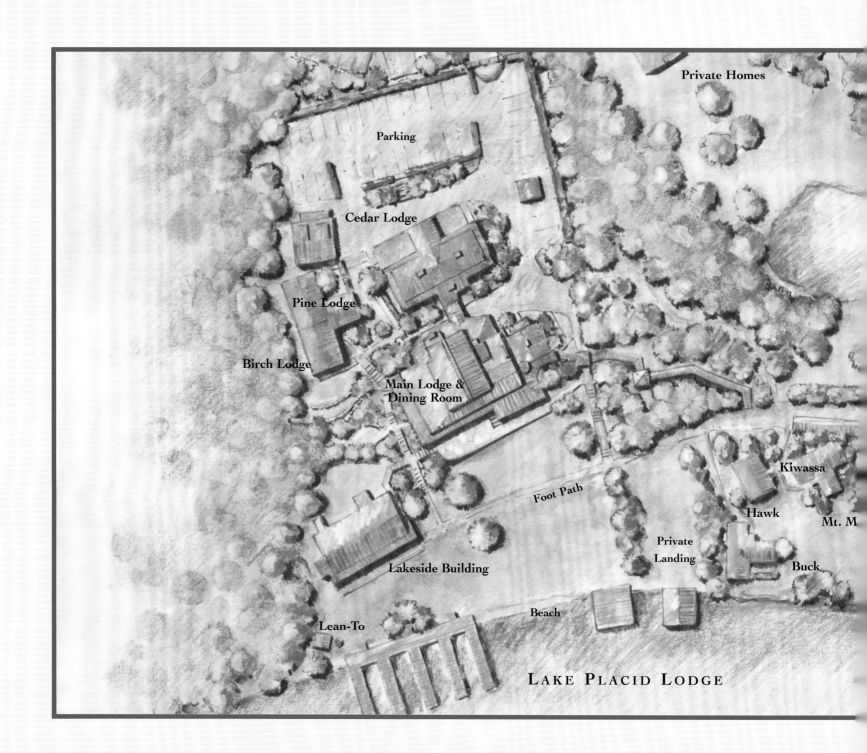

Private Homes

Parking

Cedar Lodge

Pine Lodge

Birch Lodge

Main Lodge &
Dining Room

Kiwassa

Foot Path

Hawk

Mt. M

Private
Landing

Lakeside Building

Buck

Beach

Lean-To

LAKE PLACID LODGE

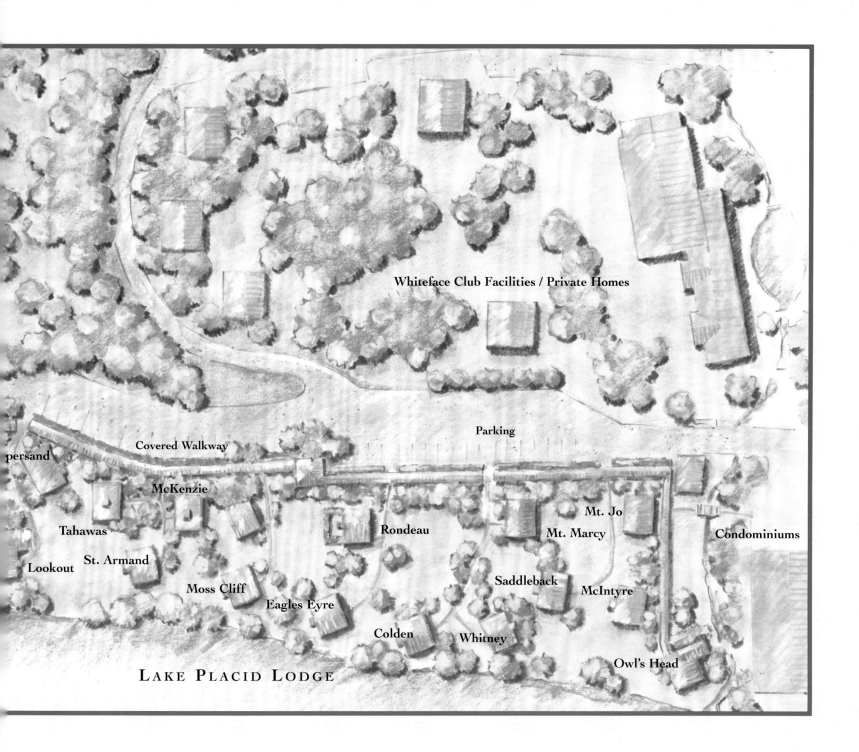

Whiteface Club Facilities / Private Homes

Parking

Covered Walkway

persand

McKenzie

Tahawas

Lookout   St. Armand

Moss Cliff

Eagles Eyre

Rondeau

Mt. Jo

Mt. Marcy

Condominiums

Saddleback

McIntyre

Colden

Whitney

Owl's Head

LAKE PLACID LODGE

43

GETTING HERE

From New York City/Albany and Points South: Take the Northway (I-87 North) to Exit 30 (Lake Placid/Keene/Saranac Lake) and follow Rte. 73 northwest into Lake Placid – about 30 miles – to a stoplight at Main Street. Turn left, go down Main Street about 1 mile to a big left (Rte. 86) between the Hilton Hotel and Ramada Inn. Go left and continue 1 1/2 miles to a road with signs for *"Lake Placid Lodge/Whiteface Club"* (this is Whiteface Inn Road, although there is no road sign). A Swiss Acres Motel is on the left. Turn right and go another 1 1/2 miles to another *"Lake Placid Lodge/ Whiteface Club"* sign. Turn right and go about 1/2 mile, following the signs through the Whiteface Club to the Lodge arch and parking lot.

From Montreal/Plattsburgh and Points North: From Montreal, take Canadian Rte. 15 and I-87 south approximately 1 hour to Exit 34 (Ausable Forks/Whiteface Mountain/Olympic Training Center). Take 9N into Ausable Forks, turning left at Stewarts, then right at the sign for Lake Placid at the end of Main Street. Continue on 9N about 10 minutes to Jay, again turning right at the sign for Lake Placid, to

Christmas at the Lodge

Wilmington's major stop sign intersection at Whiteface Mountain and "The North Pole." Turn left onto Rte. 86 toward Lake Placid. Continue about 20 minutes on Rte. 86, winding around the Ausable River, to a traffic light at Main Street in Lake Placid. Go straight down Main Street about 1 mile to the big left between the Hilton Hotel and Ramada Inn. Follow directions above to the Lodge.

From Burlington, Vermont and Points East: Driving from Vermont you must cross Lake Champlain, either by ferry or the Crown Point Bridge. The Grand Isle Ferry (Vermont to Plattsburgh, NY) runs all year and crosses every 20 minutes from 6:00 a.m. to 10:00 p.m., then every 40 minutes from 10:00 p.m. to 6:00 a.m. To get to the Grand Isle Ferry from Burlington, take I-89 north about 15 miles to Exit 17 (Rte. 2). Follow signs to the ferry landing. Once across Lake Champlain, follow signs from the ferry to I-87 south. Take I-87 south to Exit 34 (Ausable Forks/ Whiteface Mountain), about 1/2 hour. Follow directions from Montreal above.

From Syracuse and Points West: Take I-81 north to Watertown. Connect with Route 3 to Saranac Lake, then take Rte. 86 for 10 miles to a *"Welcome to Lake Placid"* sign. Just beyond (1/4 mile or so) you will see a sign on the left for *"Lake Placid Lodge/Whiteface Club"* (this is Whiteface Inn Road although there is no road sign). A Swiss Acres Motel is on the right. Turn left and go 1 1/2 miles to another *"Lake Placid Lodge/Whiteface Club"* sign. Turn right and go about 1/2 mile, following signs through the Whiteface Club, to the Lodge arch and parking lot.

"WE NEED THE TONIC OF WILDNESS. THIS CURIOUS WORLD WHICH WE INHABIT IS MORE

WONDERFUL THAN IT IS CONVENIENT, MORE BEAUTIFUL THAN IT IS USEFUL —

IT IS MORE TO BE ADMIRED AND ENJOYED THEN, THAN USED.

IN WILDNESS IS THE PRESERVATION OF THE WORLD."

Henry David Thoreau

The Adirondacks circa 1918